SEQUENTIAL
POP PIANO SONGS

20 ALL MY LOVING .... *The Beatles*

28 ALL OF ME .... *John Legend*

32 BEAUTY AND THE BEAST .... *from BEAUTY AND THE BEAST*

4   BLOWIN' IN THE WIND .... *Bob Dylan*

68 BRAVE .... *Sara Bareilles*

60 CALL ME MAYBE .... *Carly Rae Jepsen*

8   DAYDREAM BELIEVER .... *The Monkees*

44 FEEL IT STILL .... *Portugal. The Man*

48 HALLELUJAH .... *Leonard Cohen*

3   LOVE ME TENDER .... *Elvis Presley*

56 MEMORY .... *from CATS*

22 MY HEART WILL GO ON (LOVE THEME FROM 'TITANIC') .... *Celine Dion*

13 ONE CALL AWAY .... *Charlie Puth*

10 OVER THE RAINBOW .... *from THE WIZARD OF OZ*

50 PERFECT .... *Ed Sheeran*

84 RISE UP .... *Andra Day*

34 ROLLING IN THE DEEP .... *Adele*

74 SEE YOU AGAIN .... *Wiz Khalifa feat. Charlie Puth*

16 SHAKE IT OFF .... *Taylor Swift*

64 STAY WITH ME .... *Sam Smith*

39 SWEET CAROLINE .... *Neil Diamond*

25 TEARS IN HEAVEN .... *Eric Clapton*

78 THINKING OUT LOUD .... *Ed Sheeran*

6   UNCHAINED MELODY .... *Righteous Brothers*

ISBN 978-1-5400-3148-8

Visit Hal Leonard Online at
www.halleonard.com

Contact Us:
Hal Leonard
7777 West Bluemound Road
Milwaukee, WI 53213
Email: info@halleonard.com

In Europe contact:
Hal Leonard Europe Limited
42 Wigmore Street
Marylebone, London, W1U 2RN
Email: info@halleonardeurope.com

In Australia contact:
Hal Leonard Australia Pty. Ltd.
4 Lentara Court
Cheltenham, Victoria, 3192 Australia
Email: info@halleonard.com.au

The 24 songs in this book are presented in a basic order of difficulty, beginning with the easiest arrangements (hands alone, very simple rhythms) and progressing to more difficult arrangements including hands together, syncopated rhythms and moving around the keyboard.

3	LOVE ME TENDER	Elvis Presley
4	BLOWIN' IN THE WIND	Bob Dylan
6	UNCHAINED MELODY	Righteous Brothers
8	DAYDREAM BELIEVER	The Monkees
10	OVER THE RAINBOW	from THE WIZARD OF OZ
13	ONE CALL AWAY	Charlie Puth
16	SHAKE IT OFF	Taylor Swift
20	ALL MY LOVING	The Beatles
22	MY HEART WILL GO ON (LOVE THEME FROM 'TITANIC')	Celine Dion
25	TEARS IN HEAVEN	Eric Clapton
28	ALL OF ME	John Legend
32	BEAUTY AND THE BEAST	from BEAUTY AND THE BEAST
34	ROLLING IN THE DEEP	Adele
39	SWEET CAROLINE	Neil Diamond
44	FEEL IT STILL	Portugal. The Man
48	HALLELUJAH	Leonard Cohen
50	PERFECT	Ed Sheeran
56	MEMORY	from CATS
60	CALL ME MAYBE	Carly Rae Jepsen
64	STAY WITH ME	Sam Smith
68	BRAVE	Sara Bareilles
74	SEE YOU AGAIN	Wiz Khalifa feat. Charlie Puth
78	THINKING OUT LOUD	Ed Sheeran
84	RISE UP	Andra Day

LOVE ME TENDER

Words and Music by ELVIS PRESLEY
and VERA MATSON

Moderately slow

Love me ten - der, love me sweet, nev - er let me go.

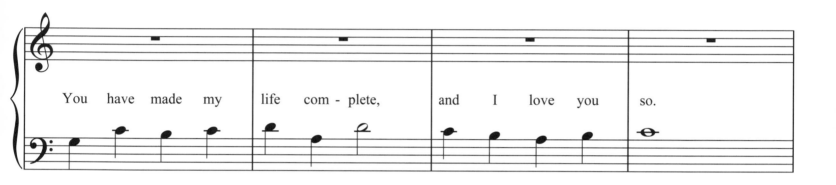

You have made my life com - plete, and I love you so.

Love me ten - der, love me true, all my dreams ful - fill.

For, my dar - lin', I love you, and I al - ways will.

BLOWIN' IN THE WIND

Words and Music by
BOB DYLAN

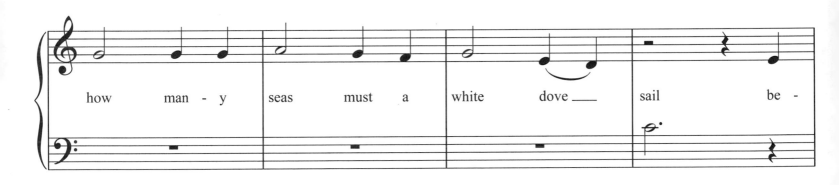

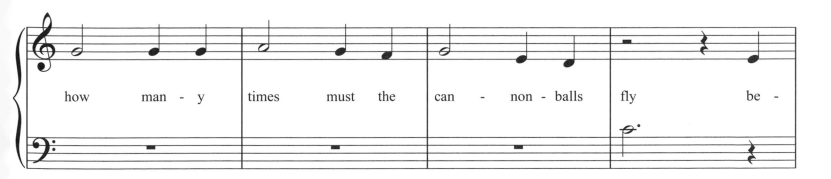

how man - y times must the can - non - balls fly be -

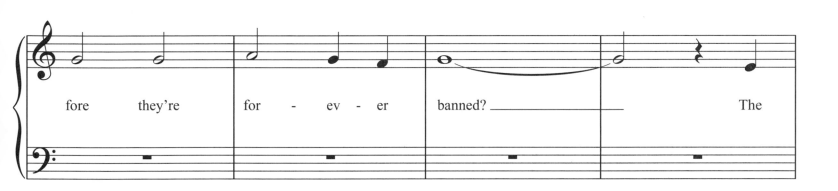

fore they're for - ev - er banned? _____ The

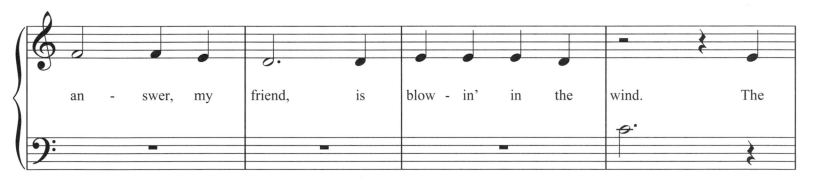

an - swer, my friend, is blow - in' in the wind. The

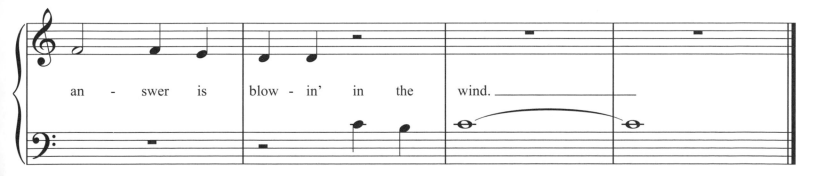

an - swer is blow - in' in the wind. _____

UNCHAINED MELODY

Lyric by HY ZARET
Music by ALEX NORTH

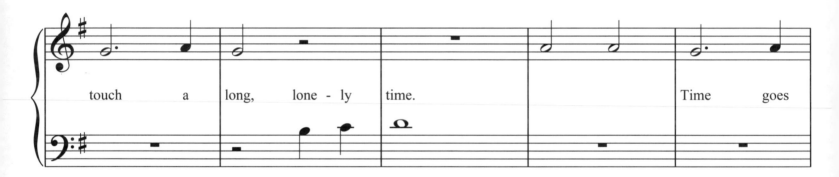

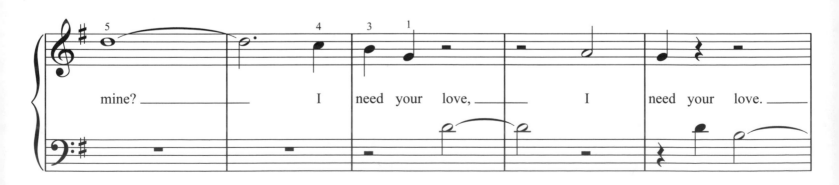

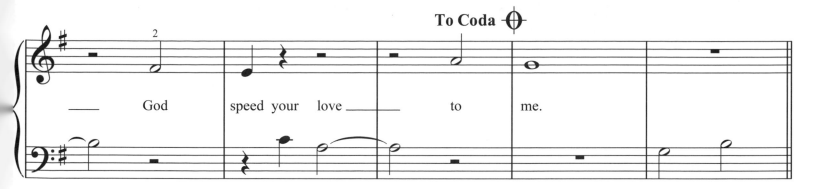

7

God speed your love ___ to me.

Lone - ly riv - ers flow to the sea, to the sea,
Lone - ly riv - ers sigh, "Wait for me, to wait for sea, me.

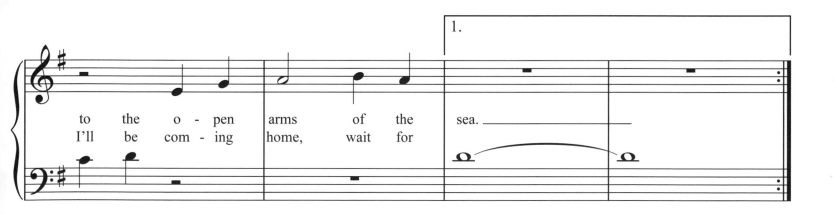

1.

to the o - pen arms of the sea. ___
I'll be com - ing home, of wait for

2.

D.C. al Coda

me!"

5

CODA

me.

DAYDREAM BELIEVER

Featured in the Television Series THE MONKEES

Words and Music by
JOHN STEWART

Moderately

Oh, I could hide 'neath the wings of the blue-bird as she

sings; the six o'-clock a - larm would nev - er

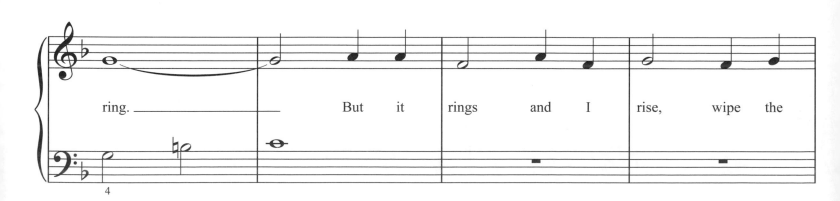

ring. ___ But it rings and I rise, wipe the

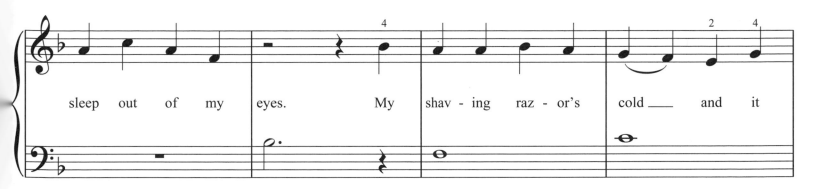

sleep out of my eyes. My shav - ing raz - or's cold ___ and it

stings. ___ Cheer up, sleep - y Jean. ___

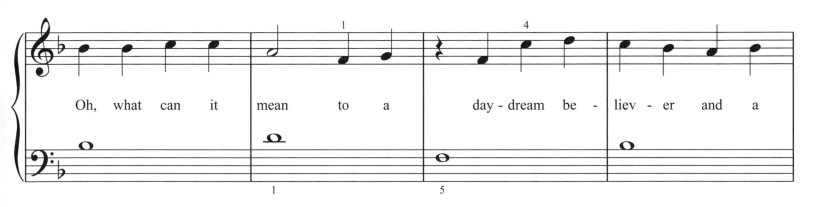

Oh, what can it mean to a day - dream be - liev - er and a

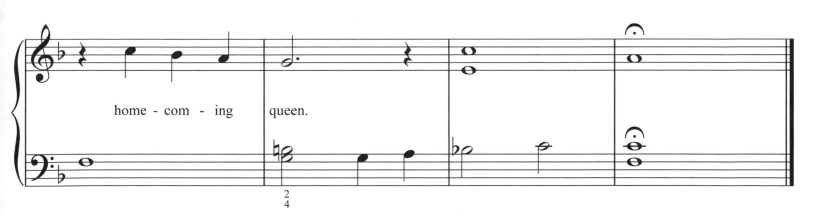

home - com - ing queen.

OVER THE RAINBOW

from THE WIZARD OF OZ

Music by HAROLD ARLEN
Lyric by E.Y. "YIP" HARBURG

Dreamily

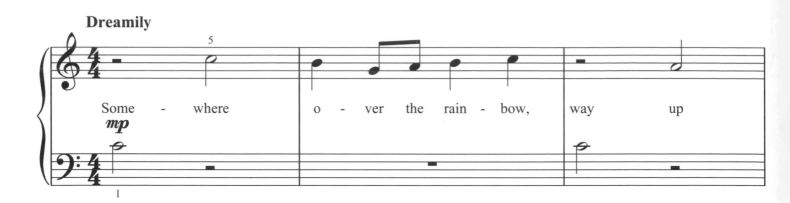

Some - where   o - ver the rain - bow,   way   up

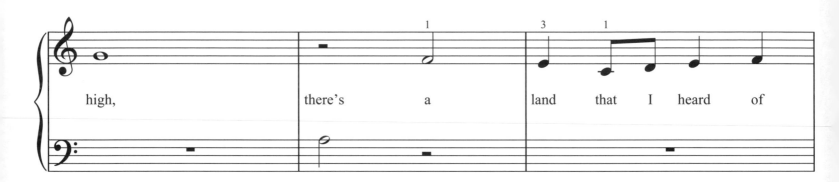

high,   there's   a   land that I   heard   of

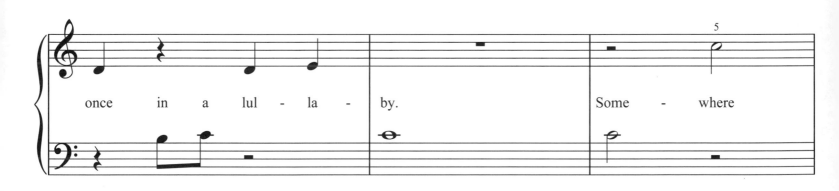

once in a lul - la - by.   Some -   where

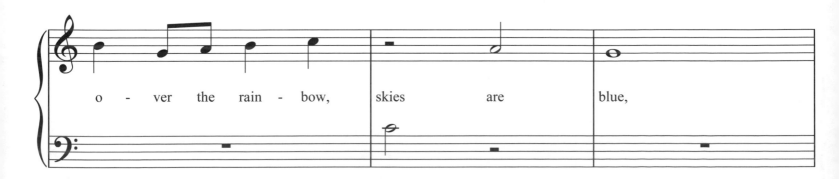

o - ver the rain - bow,   skies   are   blue,

and the dreams that you dare to dream real - ly do come

true. Some - day I'll wish up - on a star and wake up where the clouds are far be -

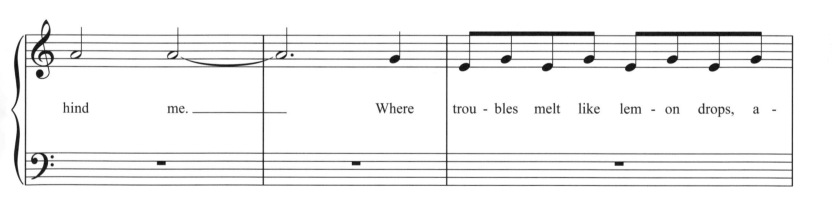

hind me. Where trou - bles melt like lem - on drops, a -

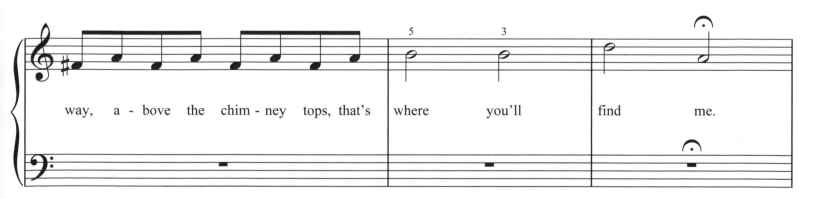

way, a - bove the chim - ney tops, that's where you'll find me.

Some - where o - ver the rain - bow blue - birds

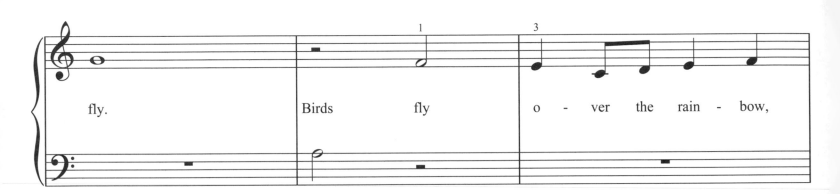

fly. Birds fly o - ver the rain - bow,

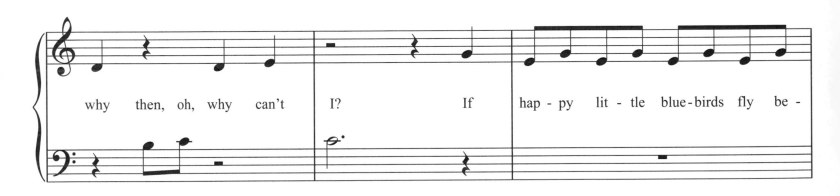

why then, oh, why can't I? If hap - py lit - tle blue-birds fly be -

yond the rain - bow, why, oh, why can't I? _____

ONE CALL AWAY

Words and Music by CHARLIE PUTH,
BREYAN ISAAC, MATT PRIME,
JUSTIN FRANKS, BLAKE ANTHONY CARTER
and MAUREEN McDONALD

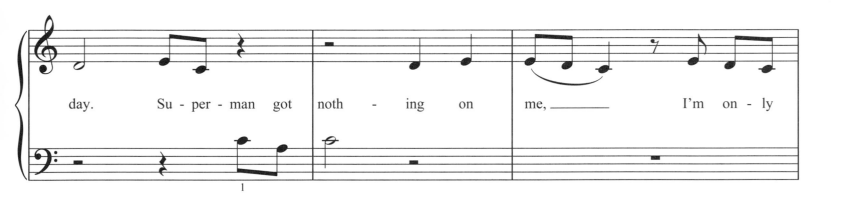

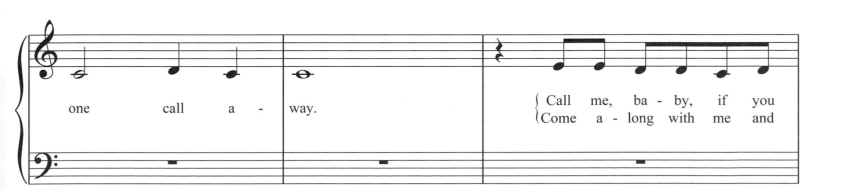

14

need   a   friend.
don't   be   scared.

I   just   wan - na   give   you
I   just   wan - na   set   you

love.   Come   on,   come   on,   come
free.   Come   on,   come   on,   come

on.   Reach - ing   out   to   you,   so
on.   You   and   me   can   make   it

1.

take   a   chance.   No
an - y - where.   For

mat - ter   where   you   go,

2.

know you're not a - lone. I'm on - ly

now, we can stay here for a   while   'cause, you

know, I just wan - na see you smile. _____ No mat - ter where you go, you

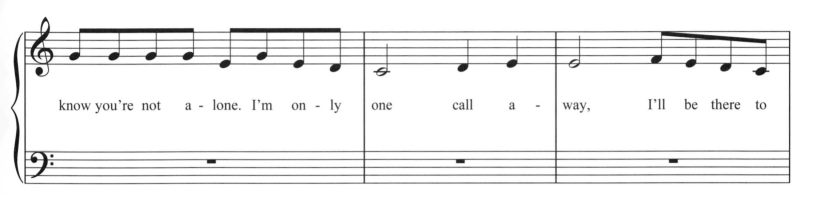

know you're not a - lone. I'm on - ly one call a - way, I'll be there to

save the day. Su - per - man got noth - ing on

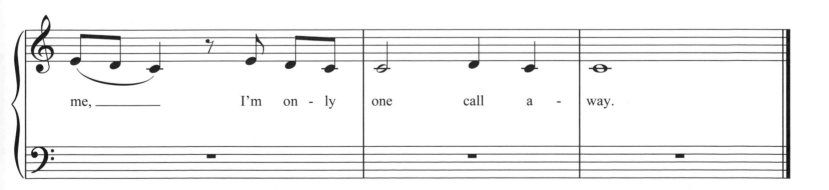

me, _____ I'm on - ly one call a - way.

SHAKE IT OFF

Words and Music by TAYLOR SWIFT,
MAX MARTIN and SHELLBACK

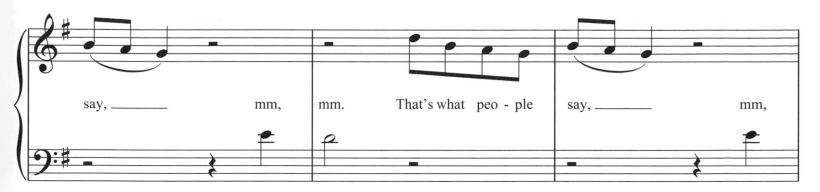

say, _____ mm, mm. That's what peo - ple say, _____ mm,

mm. But I keep cruis - ing; can't stop, won't stop

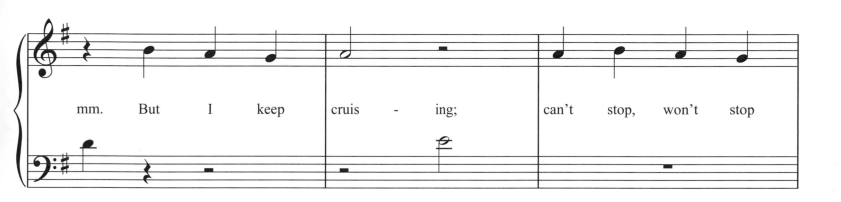

mov - ing. It's like I got this mu - sic

in my mind say - ing, "It's gon - na be al - right." 'Cause the

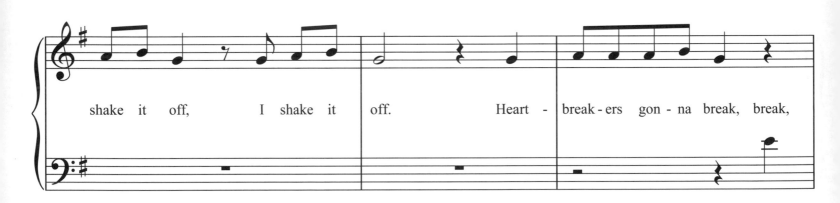

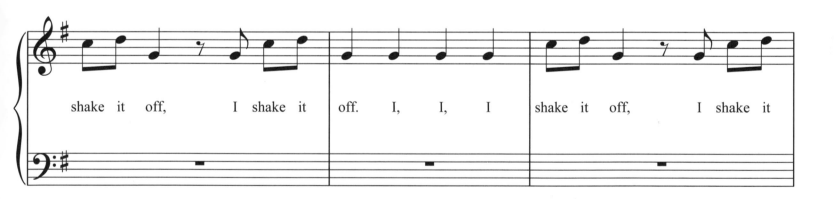

ALL MY LOVING

Words and Music by JOHN LENNON
and PAUL McCARTNEY

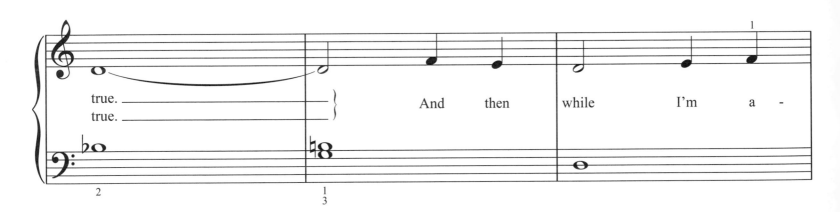

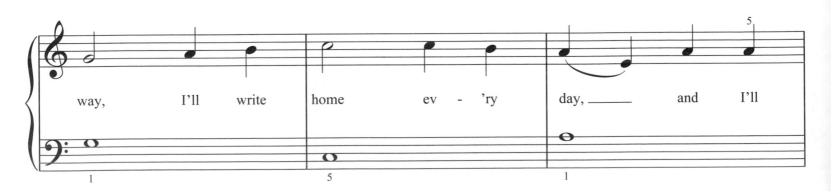

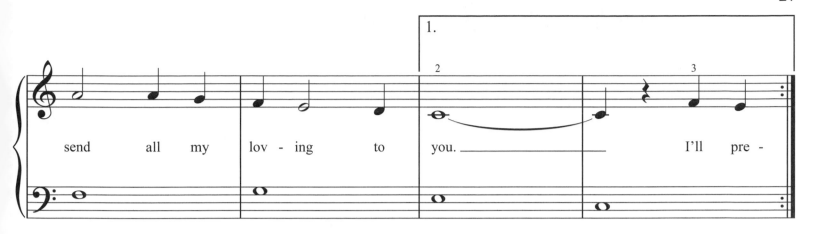

send all my lov - ing to you. I'll pre -

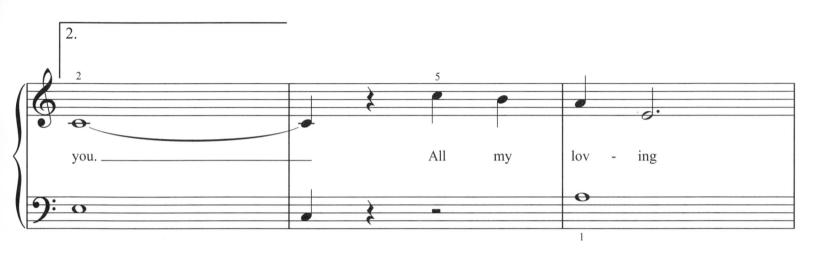

you. All my lov - ing

I will send to you, all my

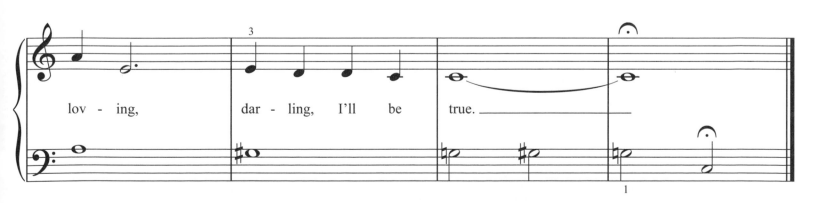

lov - ing, dar - ling, I'll be true.

MY HEART WILL GO ON

(Love Theme from 'Titanic')

from the Paramount and Twentieth Century Fox Motion Picture TITANIC

Music by JAMES HORNER
Lyric by WILL JENNINGS

Ev - 'ry night in my dreams I see you, I

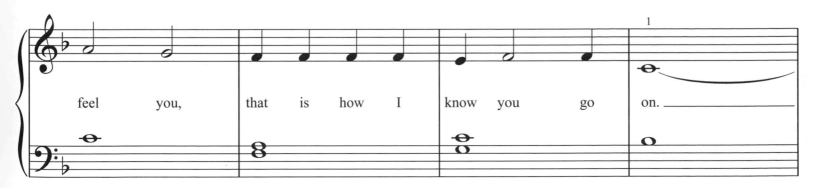

feel   you,   that   is   how   I   know   you   go   on. _____

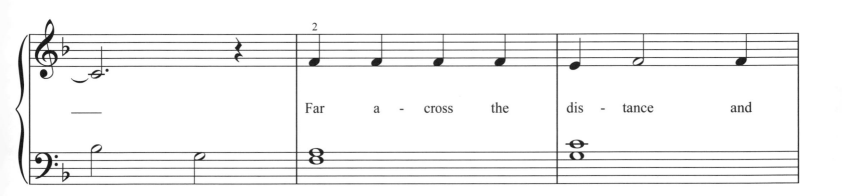

_____   Far   a - cross   the   dis - tance   and

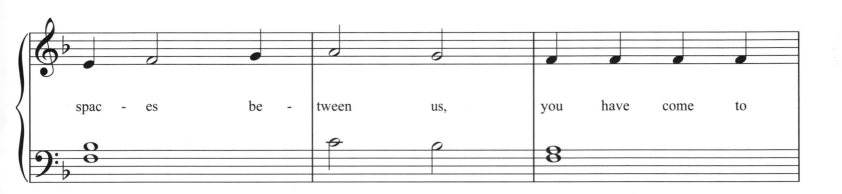

spac - es   be - tween   us,   you   have   come   to

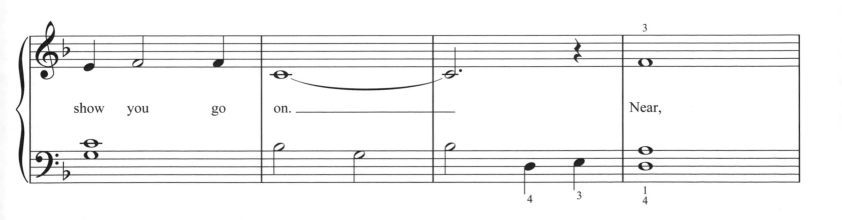

show   you   go   on. _____   Near,

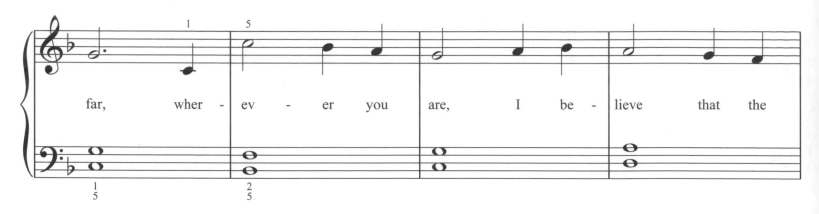

far, wher - ev - er you are, I be - lieve that the

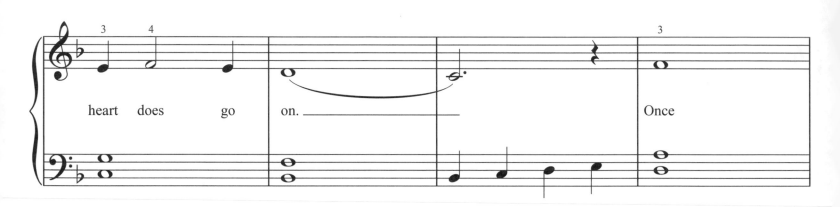

heart does go on. _____ Once

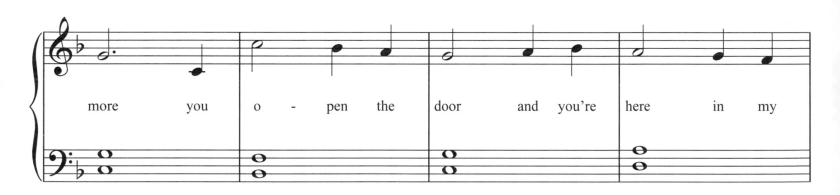

more you o - pen the door and you're here in my

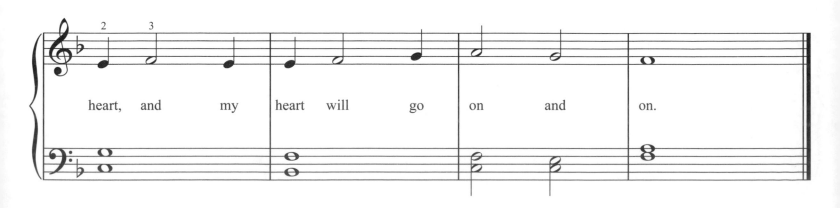

heart, and my heart will go on and on.

TEARS IN HEAVEN

Words and Music by ERIC CLAPTON
and WILL JENNINGS

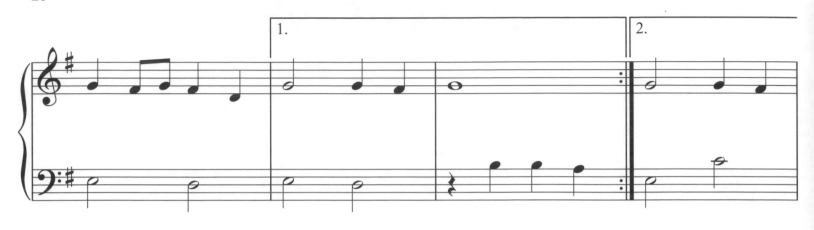

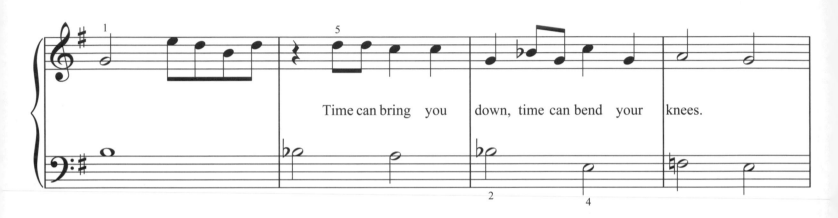

Time can bring you down, time can bend your knees.

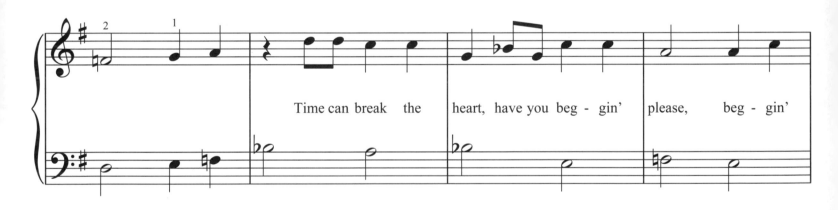

Time can break the heart, have you beg - gin' please, beg - gin'

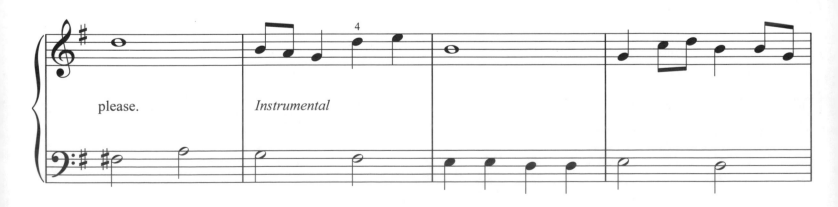

please. *Instrumental*

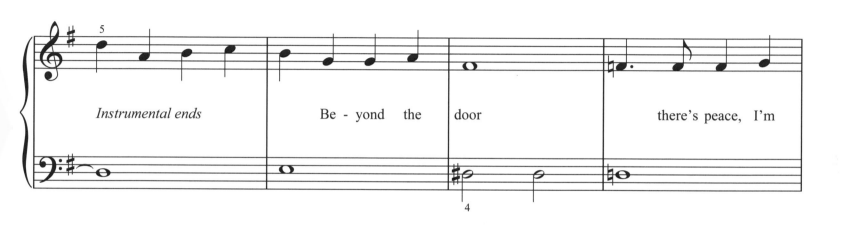

Instrumental ends   Be - yond the   door   there's peace, I'm

D.C. al Coda
(verse 1)

sure.   And I   know there'll be   no more _____ tears in heav - en.

CODA

en.   rit.

ALL OF ME

Words and Music by JOHN STEPHENS
and TOBY GAD

Moderately, with feeling

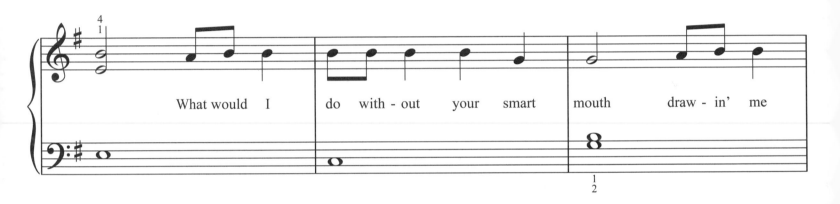

What would I do with-out your smart mouth draw-in' me

in and you kick-ing me out? You've got my head spin-nin',

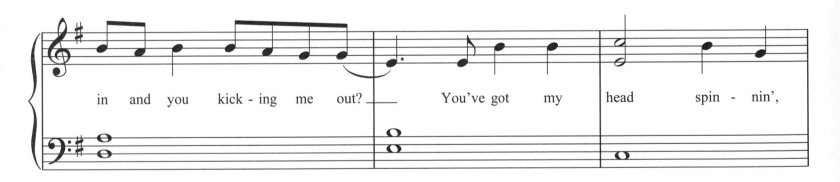

no kid-din'. I can't pin you down. What's go-in'

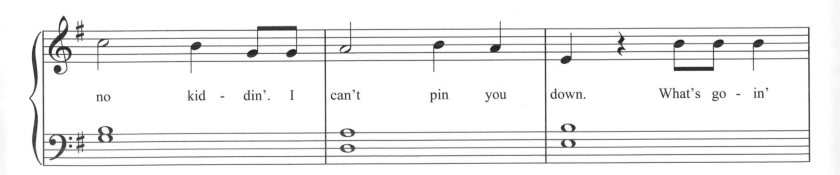

on in that beau - ti - ful mind? I'm on your mag - i - cal mys - ter - y ride. __

__ And I'm so diz - zy; don't know what hit me. But

I'll be al - right. My head's un - der

wa - ter, _____ but I'm breath - ing fine.

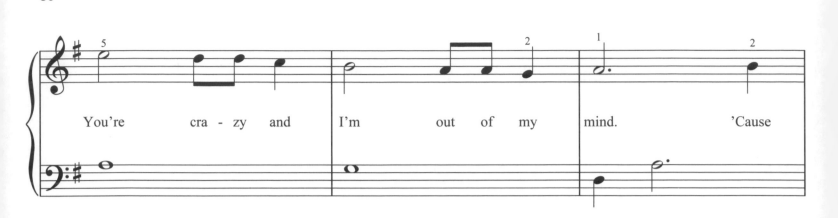

You're   cra - zy   and   I'm   out   of   my   mind.   'Cause

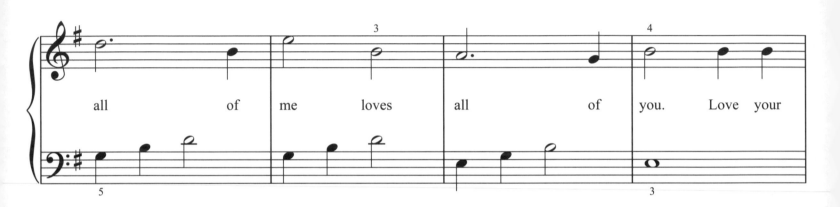

all   of   me   loves   all   of   you.   Love   your

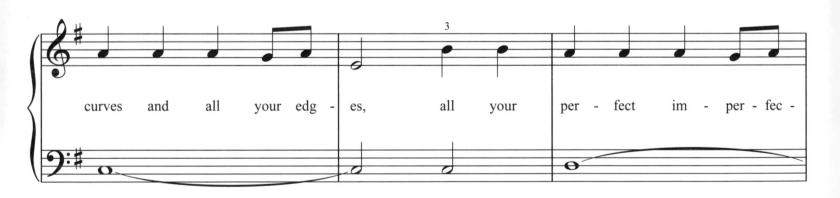

curves   and   all   your   edg -   es,   all   your   per - fect   im - per - fec -

tions.   Give   your   all   to   me,   I'll   give   my   all   to

31

you.　　You're　my　　end　　and　　my　　be - gin - ning.　　E - ven

when　I　lose,　I'm　win - ning.　'Cause　I　give　you　all _____

_____　of　me,　　　　and　you　give　me

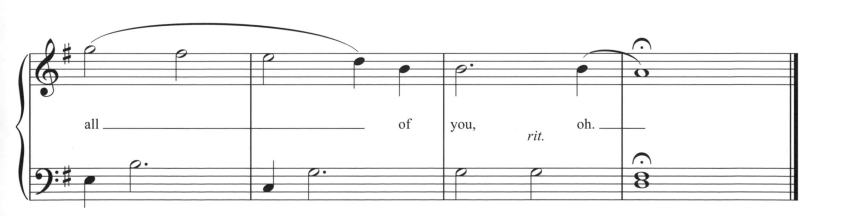

all _____　of　you,　oh. ____

rit.

BEAUTY AND THE BEAST

from BEAUTY AND THE BEAST

Music by ALAN MENKEN
Lyrics by HOWARD ASHMAN

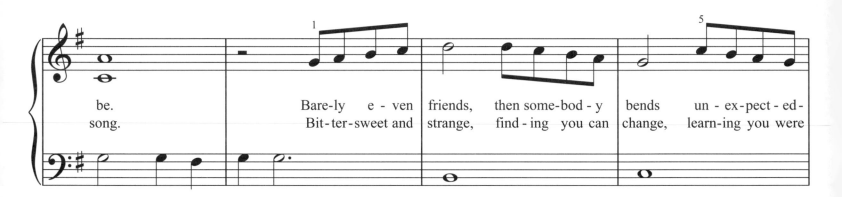

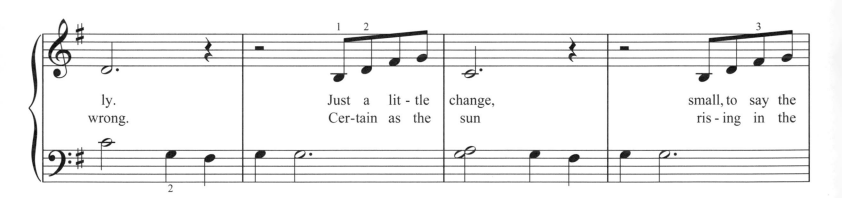

ROLLING IN THE DEEP

Words and Music by ADELE ADKINS
and PAUL EPWORTH

Soul groove

There's a fire _____ start-ing in my heart, reach-ing a fe - ver pitch and

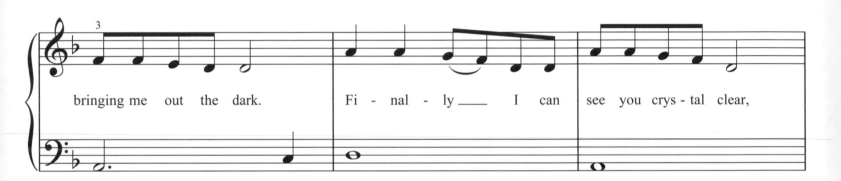

bringing me out the dark. Fi - nal - ly _____ I can see you crys - tal clear,

go a - head and sell me out and I'll lay your ship bare.

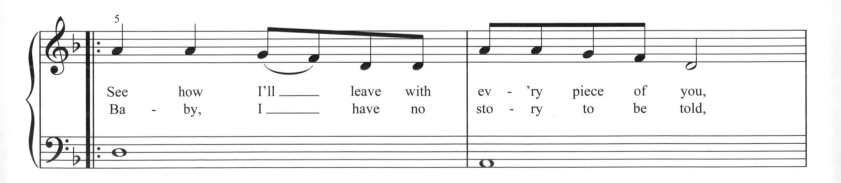

See how I'll _____ leave with ev - 'ry piece of you,
Ba - by, I _____ have no sto - ry to be told,

don't un - der - es - ti - mate the things that I will do.
I've heard _____ one on you. I'm gonna make your head burn.

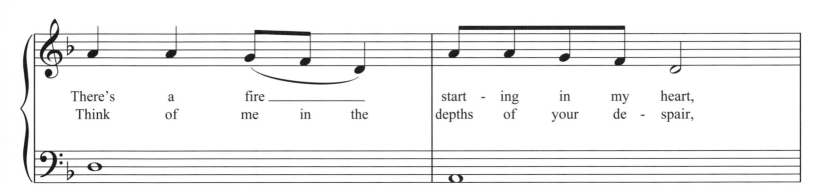

There's a fire _____ start - ing in my heart,
Think of me in the depths of your de - spair,

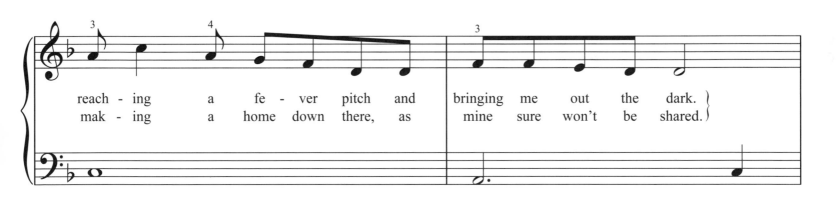

reach - ing a fe - ver pitch and bringing me out the dark.
mak - ing a home down there, as mine sure won't be shared.

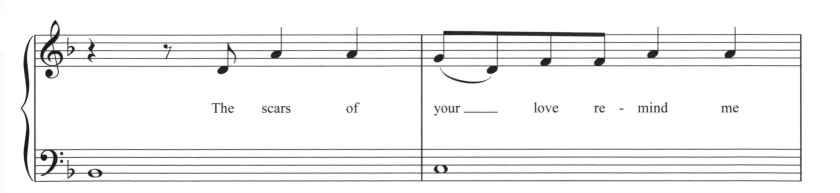

The scars of your _____ love re - mind me

of _____ us, they keep me think - ing that we al - most had it

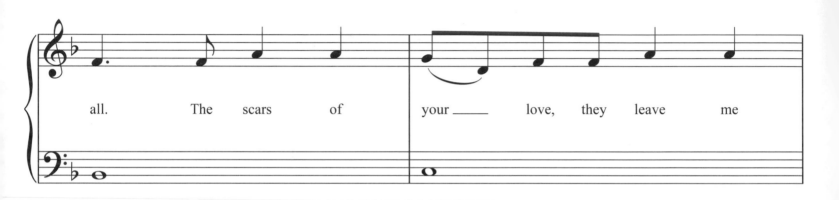

all. The scars of your _____ love, they leave me

breath - less, I can't help feel - ing we could have had it

all, _____ roll - ing in the deep. _____

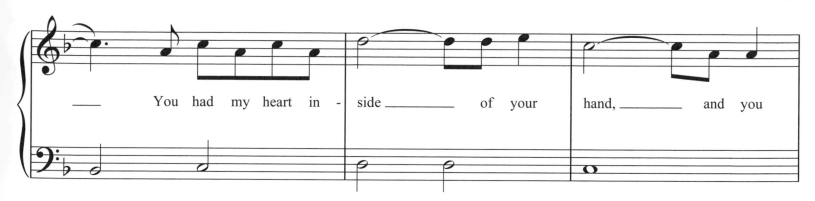

You had my heart in - side _____ of your hand, _____ and you

played it to the beat. _____

1.

_____

2.

_____ We could have had it

all. _____ Roll - ing in the deep. _____

_____ You had my heart in - side _____ of your hand, _____ and you

played it to the beat. ___ We could have had it all. ___

___ Roll - ing in the deep. ___ You had my heart in -

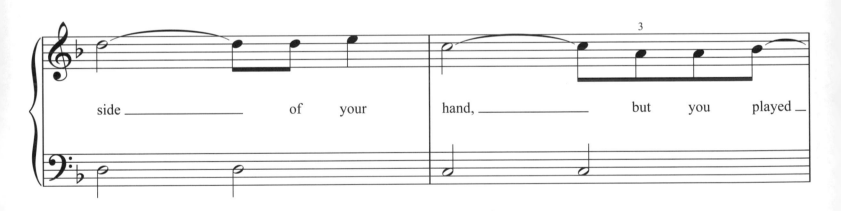

side ___ of your hand, ___ but you played ___

___ it, you played ___ it, you played ___ it, you played ___ it to the beat. ___

SWEET CAROLINE

Words and Music by
NEIL DIAMOND

40

and spring be - came the sum - mer.　Who'd have be - lieved you'd come a -

long?　　Hands, _____　Warm, _____

touch - in' hands,　　reach - in' out,
touch - in' warm,

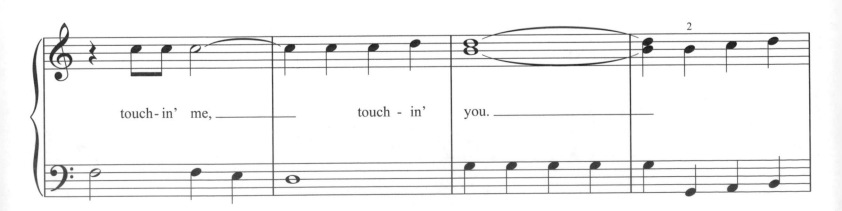

touch - in' me, _____　touch - in'　you. _____

Sweet   Car - o - line, ___   good times nev - er seemed so

good. _____   I've   been in - clined ___

To Coda ⊕

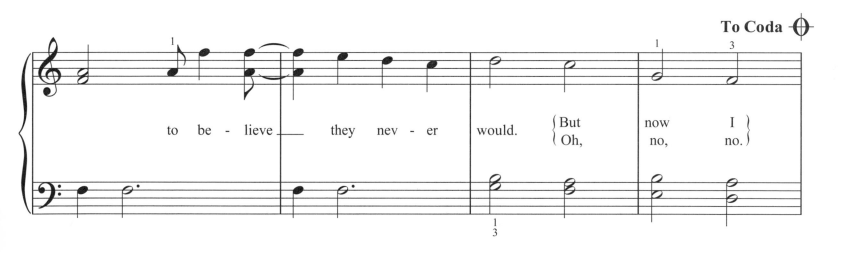

to be - lieve ___ they nev - er   would.   {But   now   I }
{Oh,   no,   no.}

look at the   night,   and it don't   seem so lone - ly.

42

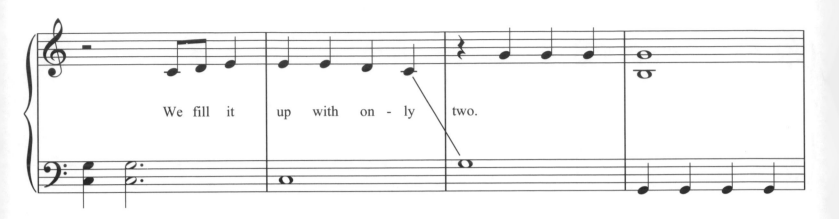

We fill it up with on - ly two.

And when I hurt, hurt- in' runs off my shoul - ders.

D.S. al Coda

How can I hurt when hold - in' you?

CODA

Sweet   Car - o - line, _

good times nev - er seemed so   good. _____

I've   been in - clined ___   to be - lieve _

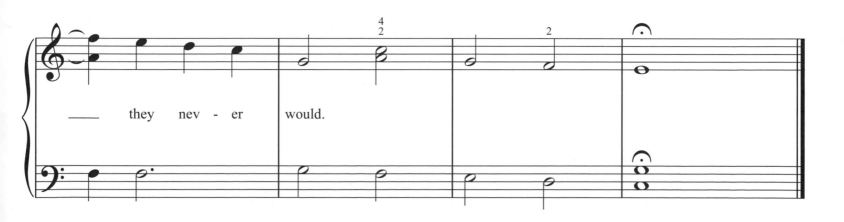

they nev - er   would.

FEEL IT STILL

Words and Music by JOHN GOURLEY, ZACH CAROTHERS,
JASON SECHRIST, ERIC HOWK, KYLE O'QUIN,
BRIAN HOLLAND, FREDDIE GORMAN, GEORGIA DOBBINS,
ROBERT BATEMAN, WILLIAM GARRETT, JOHN HILL
and ASA TACCONE

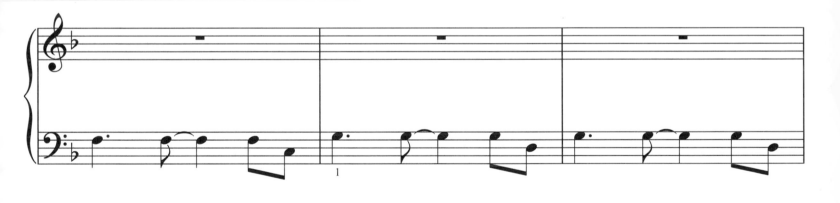

Can't keep my hands to my-self.

45

Think I'll dust 'em off, put 'em back up on the shelf, __

__ case my lit - tle ba - by girl is in need. __ Am I

com - ing out - ta left field? Ooh, ____ I'm a reb - el just for kicks, now.

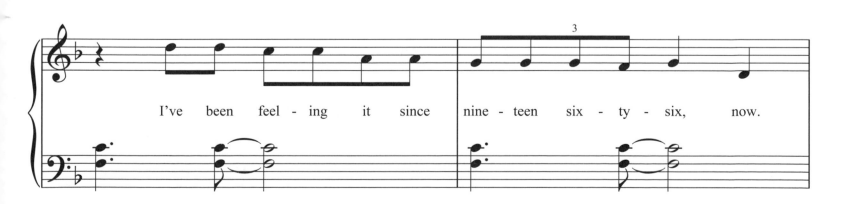

I've been feel - ing it since nine - teen six - ty - six, now.

Might be o - ver ___ now, but I feel it still.

Ooh, ___ I'm a reb - el just for kicks, now.

Let me kick it like it's nine - teen eight - y - six, now.

Might be o - ver ___ now, but I feel it still.

Ooh, _____ I'm a

reb - el just for kicks, now. I've been feel - ing it since

nine-teen six - ty - six, now. Might be o - ver _____ now, but I feel it still. _____

_____ Might have had your fill, but you feel it still. _____

HALLELUJAH

Words and Music by
LEONARD COHEN

Moderately slow, in 2

heard there was a se - cret chord ___ that Da - vid played, ___ and it

pleased the Lord, ___ but you don't ___ real - ly care for mu - sic,

do you? ___ It goes like this: the fourth, the fifth, the

minor fall, ___ the ma - jor lift, ___ the baf - fled king ___ com - pos - ing ___ Hal - le -

lu - jah. ___ Hal - le - lu - jah, ___ Hal - le -

lu - jah, ___ Hal - le - lu - jah, ___ Hal - le -

lu - jah. ___

8vb

PERFECT

Words and Music by
ED SHEERAN

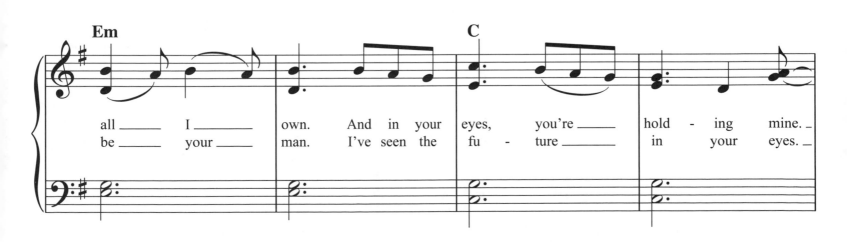

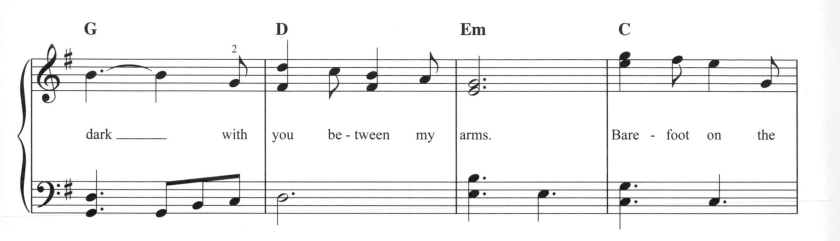

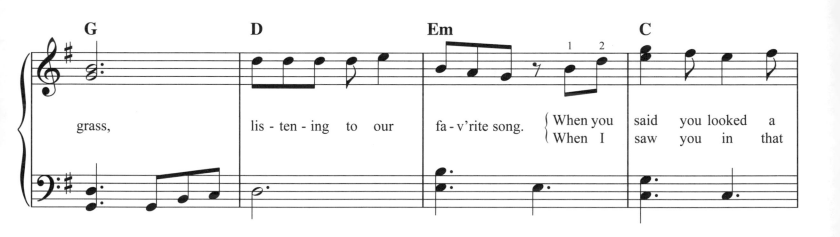

you look per - fect to - night. ____
you look per - fect to - night. ____

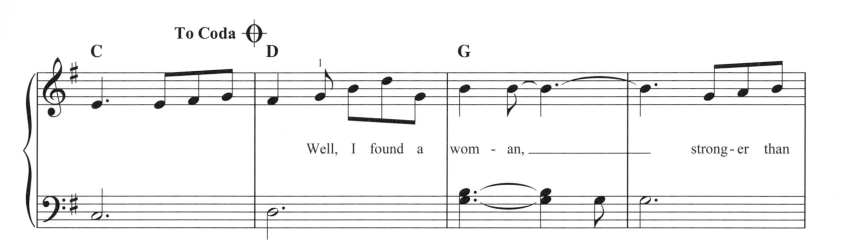

Well, I found a wom - an, _____ strong - er than

an - y - one I know. ____ She shares my dreams, I hope __ that some - day, I'll share her

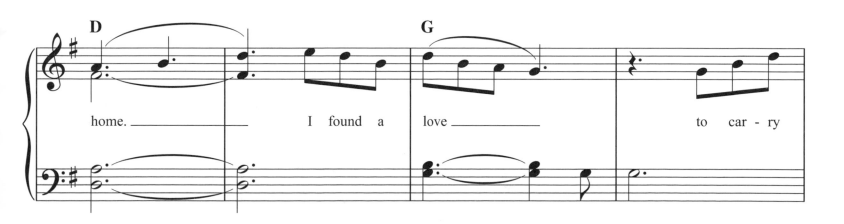

home. _____ I found a love _____ to car - ry

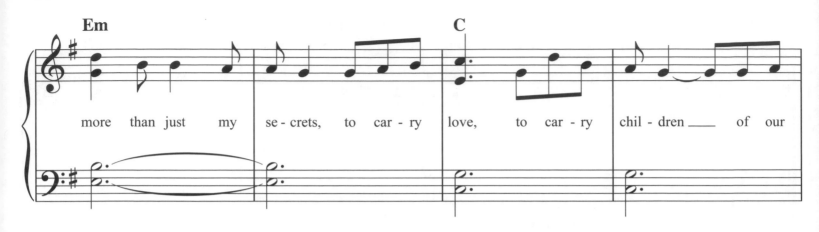

Em ... **C**

more than just my se-crets, to car-ry love, to car-ry chil-dren _____ of our

D ... D.S. al Coda ... **CODA** ... **D**

own. _____ We are still kids, but we're

Ba - by, _____

Em ... **C** ... **G** ... **D**

I'm _____ danc - ing in the dark _____ with you be - tween my

Em ... **C** ... **G** ... **D**

arms. Bare - foot on the grass, lis - ten - ing to our

55

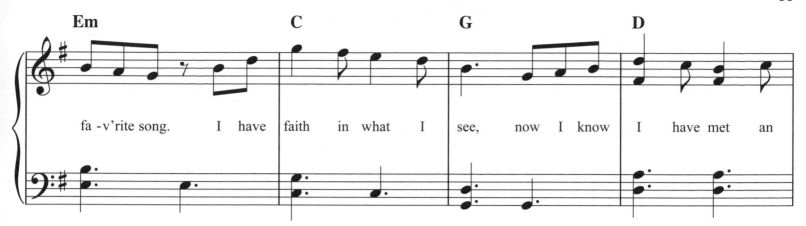

fa -v'rite song.   I have faith in what I   see,   now I know   I   have met an

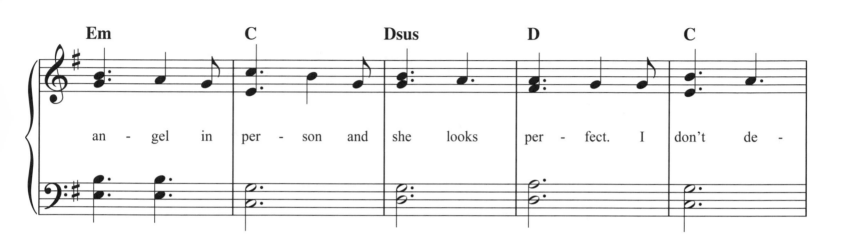

an - gel   in per - son and she   looks   per - fect.   I   don't de -

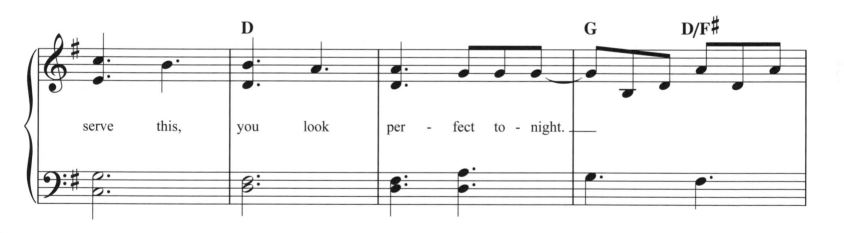

serve   this,   you   look   per - fect to - night. ___

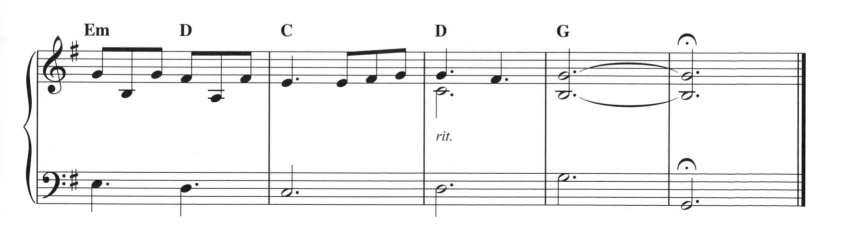

rit.

MEMORY
from CATS

Music by ANDREW LLOYD WEBBER
Text by TREVOR NUNN after T.S. ELIOT

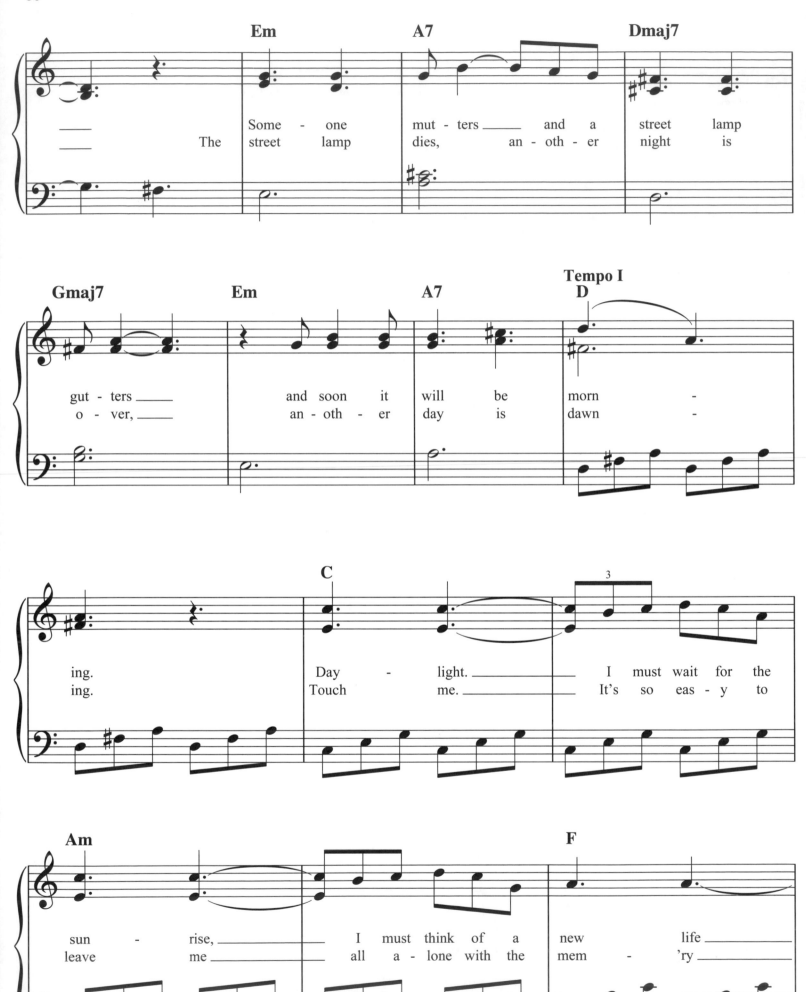

59

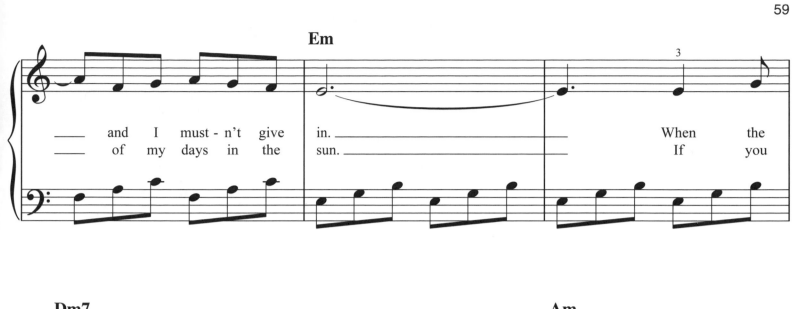

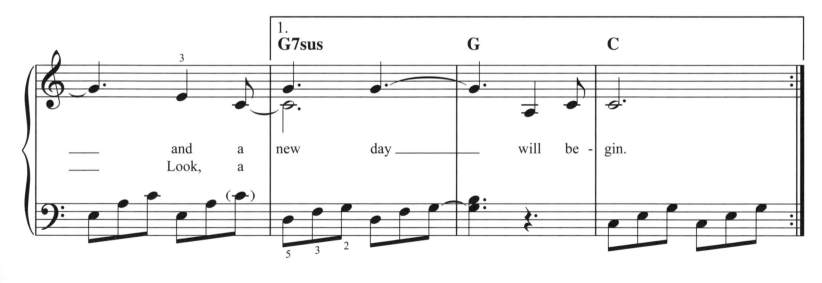

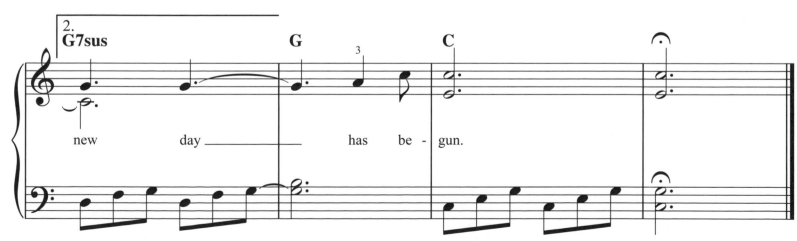

CALL ME MAYBE

Words and Music by CARLY RAE JEPSEN,
JOSHUA RAMSAY and TAVISH CROWE

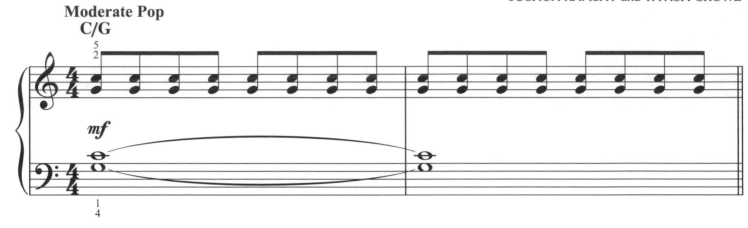

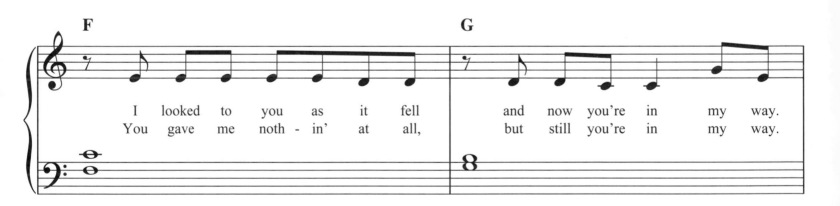

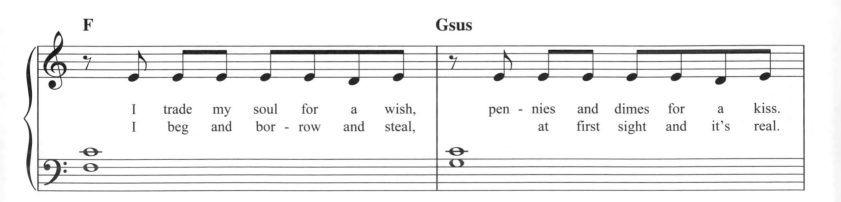

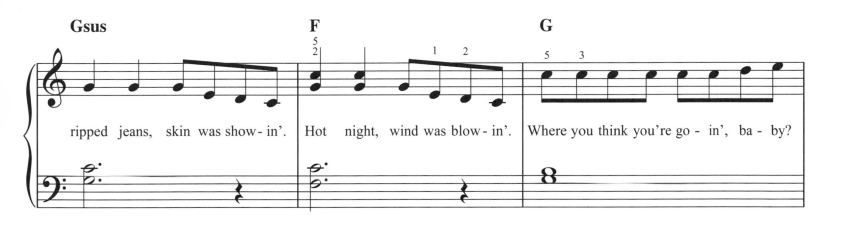

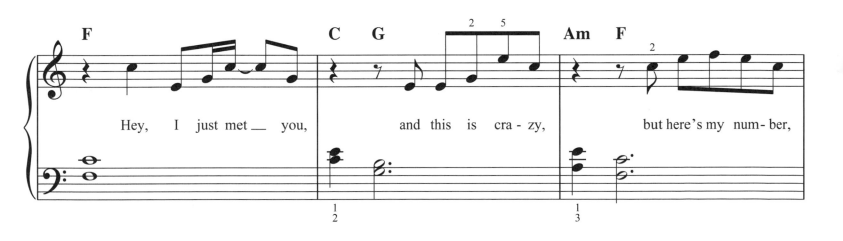

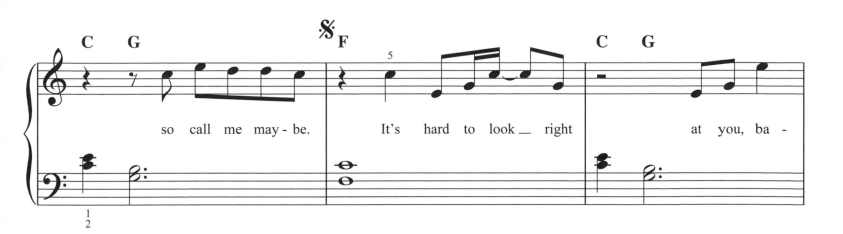

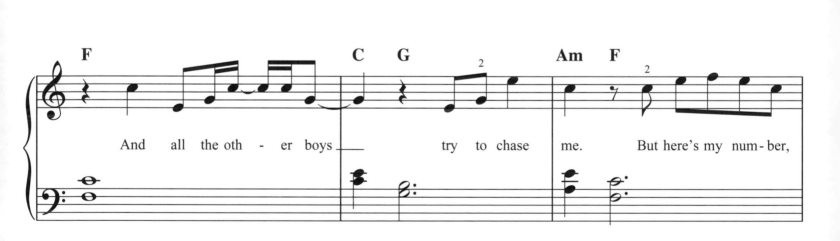

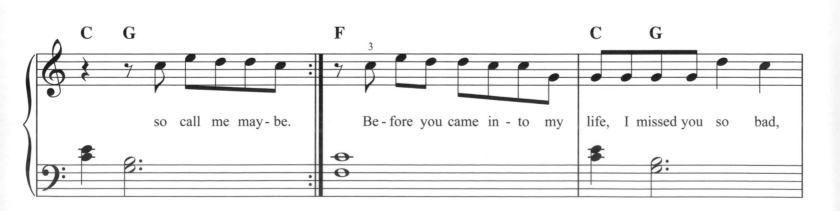

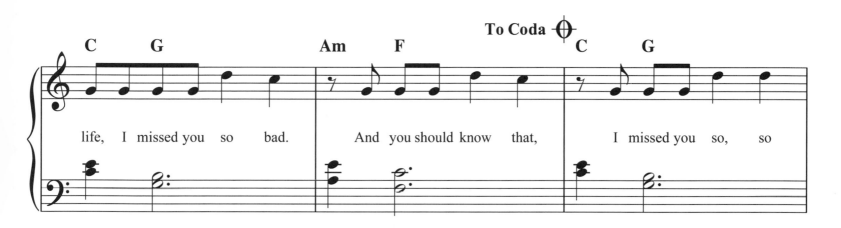

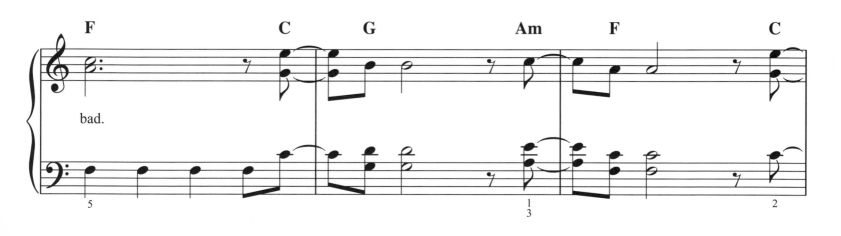

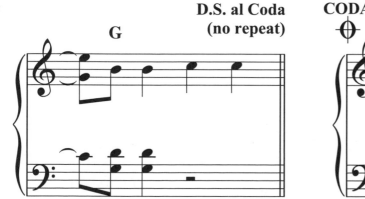

STAY WITH ME

Words and Music by SAM SMITH,
JAMES NAPIER, WILLIAM EDWARD PHILLIPS,
TOM PETTY and JEFF LYNNE

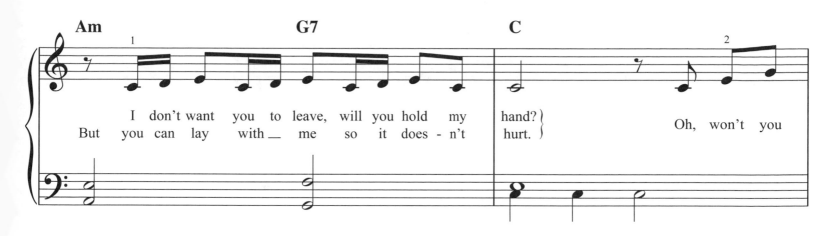

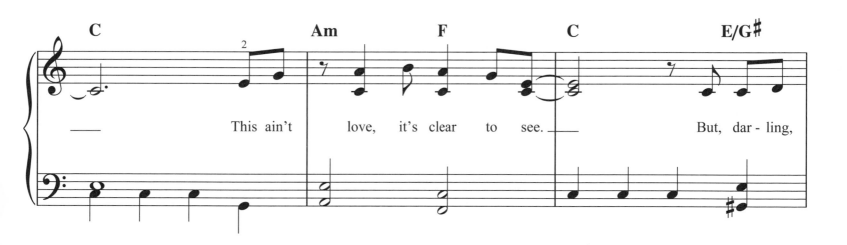

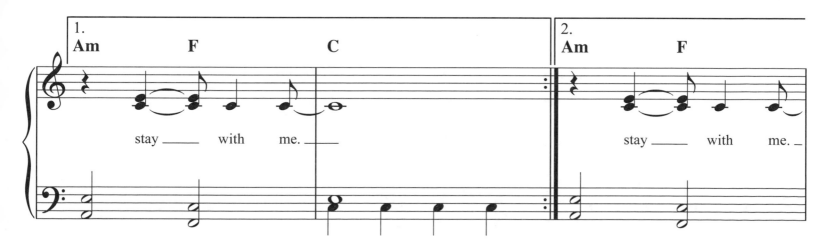

love, it's clear _____ to see. But, dar-ling, stay _____ with me.

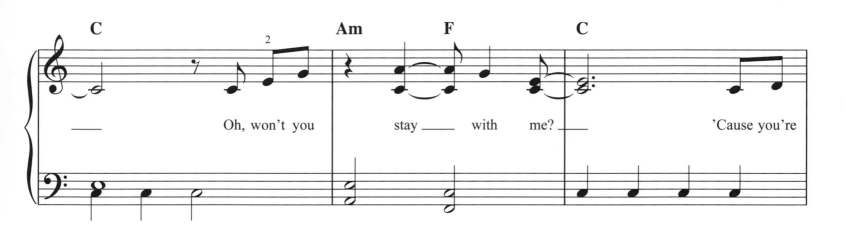

____ Oh, won't you stay ____ with me? ____ 'Cause you're

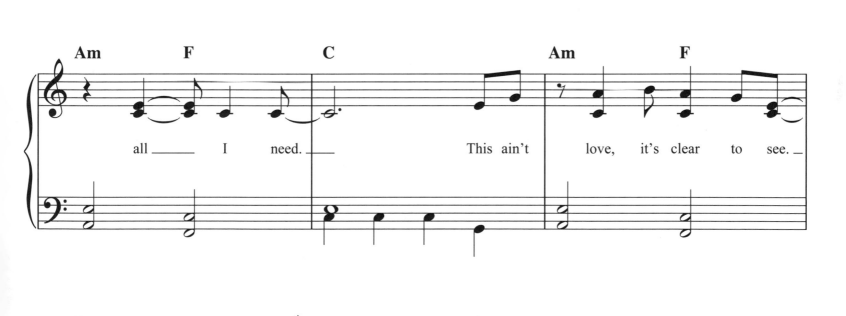

all ____ I need. ____ This ain't love, it's clear to see. ____

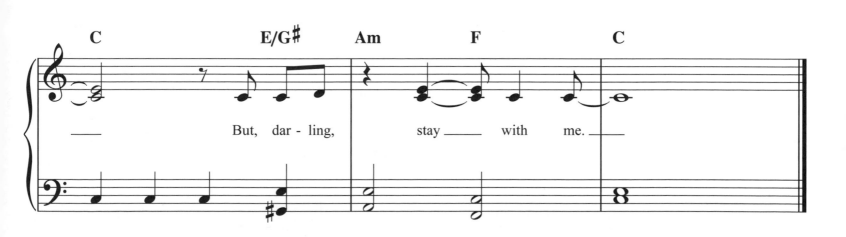

____ But, dar-ling, stay ____ with me. ____

BRAVE

Words and Music by SARA BAREILLES
and JACK ANTONOFF

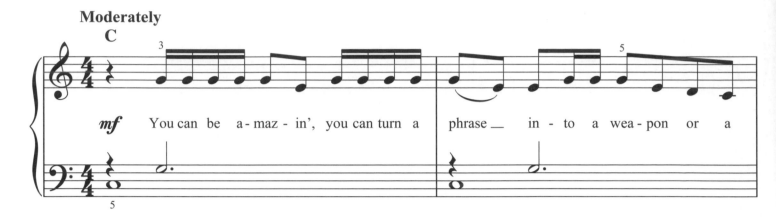

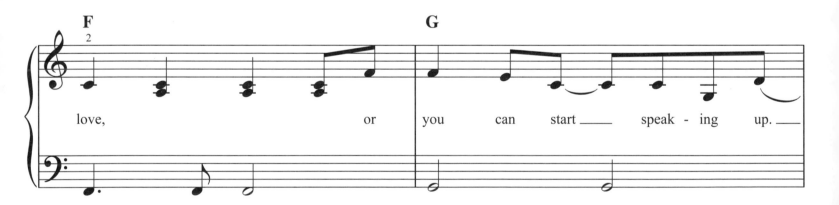

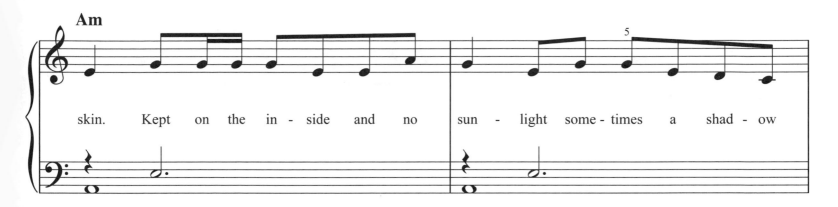

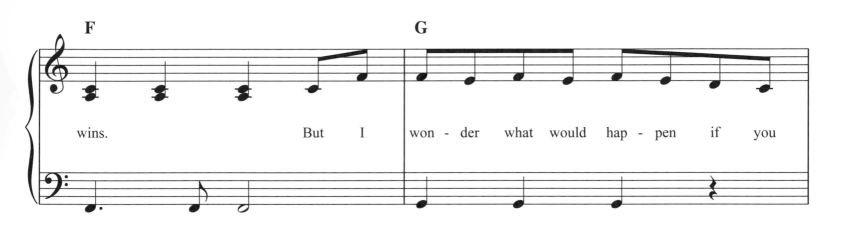

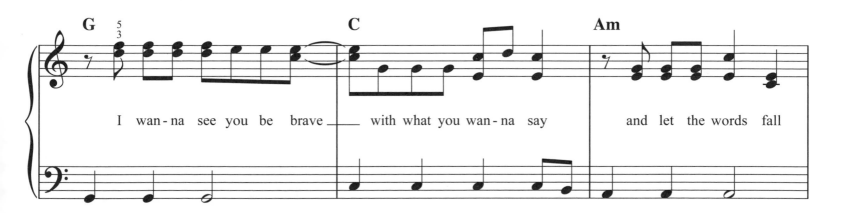

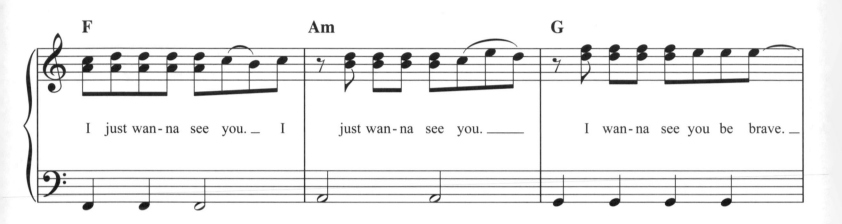

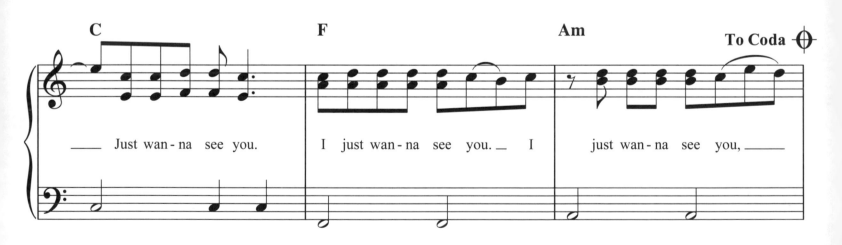

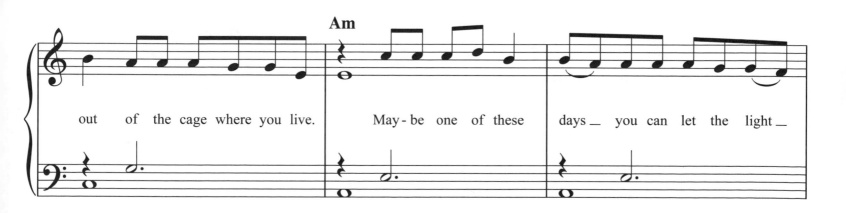

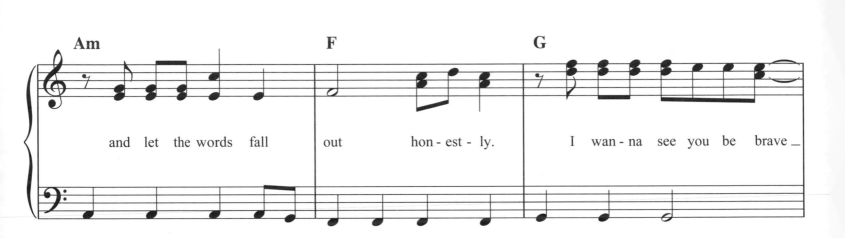

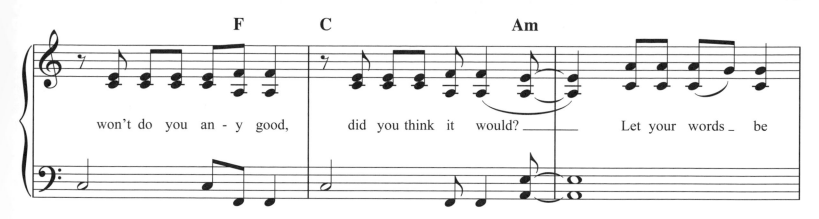

SEE YOU AGAIN

from FURIOUS 7

Words and Music by CAMERON THOMAZ,
CHARLIE PUTH, JUSTIN FRANKS,
ANDREW CEDAR, DANN HUME,
JOSH HARDY and PHOEBE COCKBURN

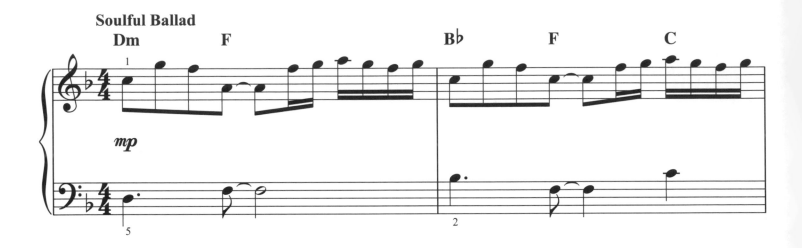

see you a - gain. ____ We've come a long way ____ from

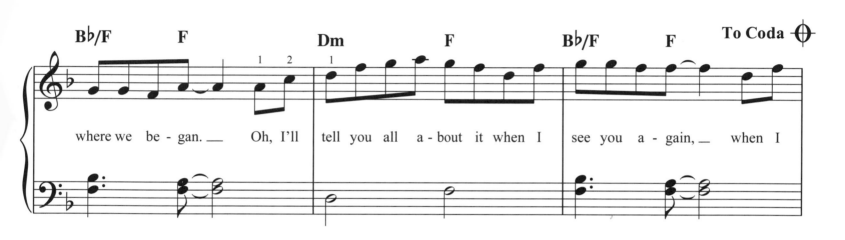

where we be - gan. ___ Oh, I'll tell you all a - bout it when I see you a - gain, __ when I

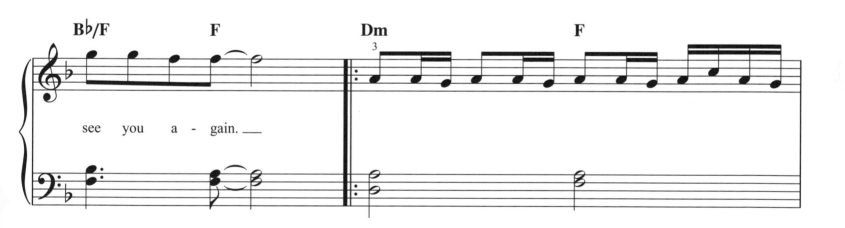

see you a - gain. ___

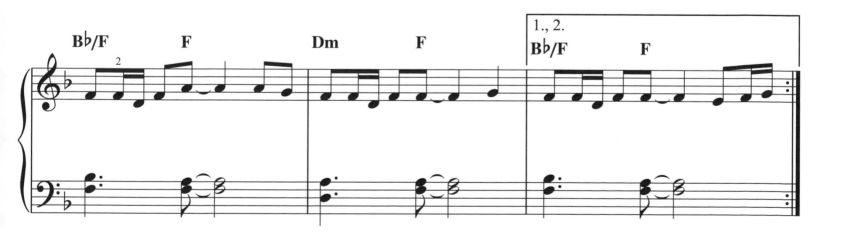

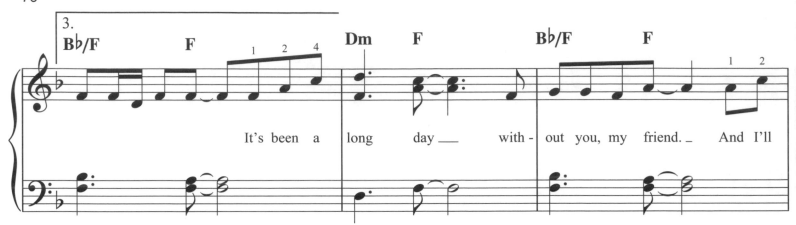

It's been a long day ___ with- out you, my friend. _ And I'll

tell you all a - bout it when I see you a - gain. ___ We've come a

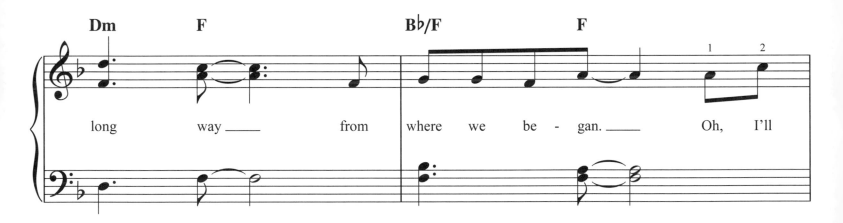

long way ___ from where we be - gan. ___ Oh, I'll

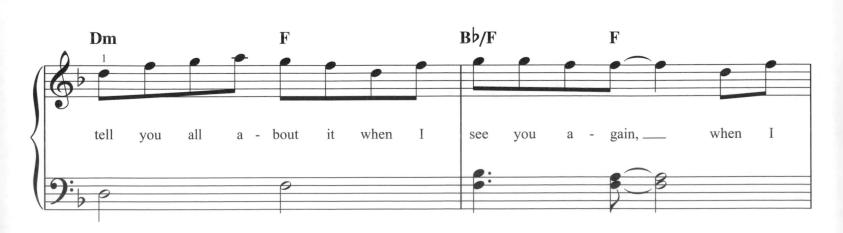

tell you all a - bout it when I see you a - gain, ___ when I

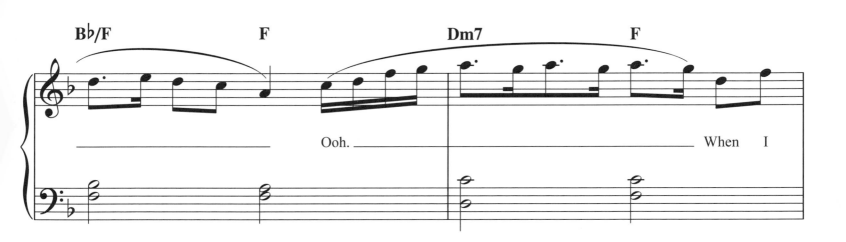

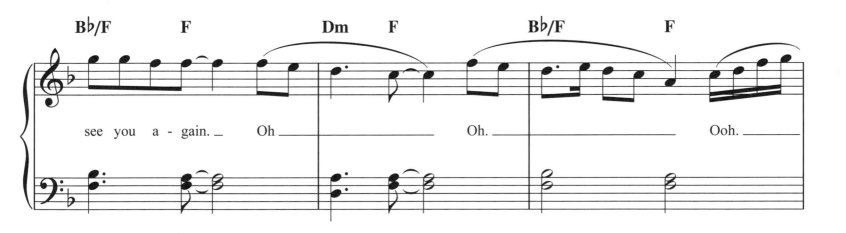

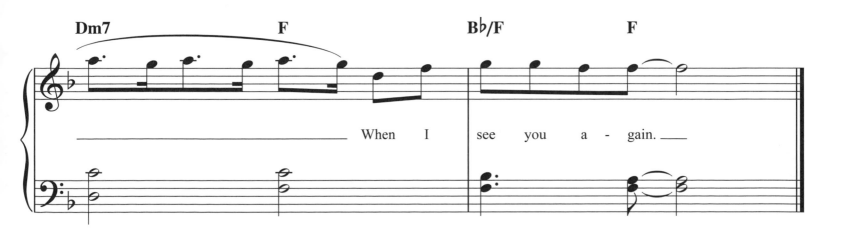

THINKING OUT LOUD

Words and Music by ED SHEERAN
and AMY WADGE

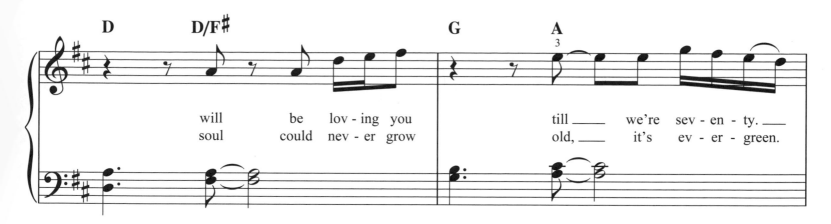

will   be   lov - ing   you   till ____ we're   sev - en - ty. ____
soul   could   nev - er   grow   old, ____   it's   ev - er - green.

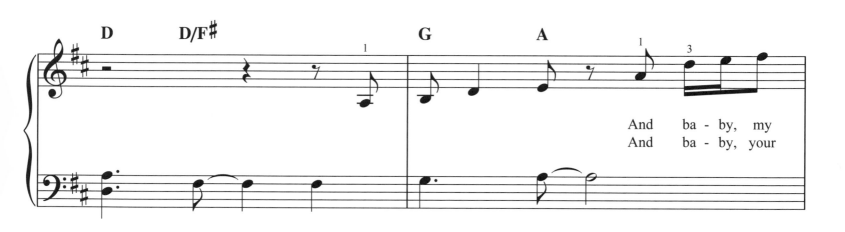

And   ba - by,   my
And   ba - by,   your

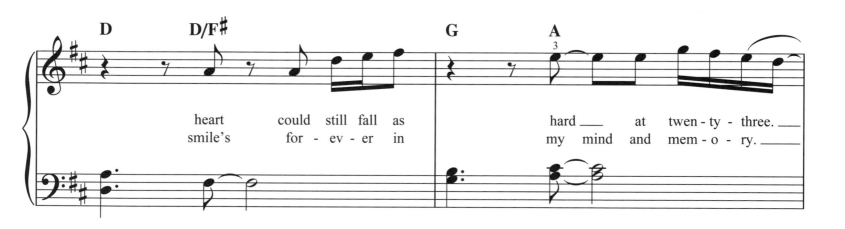

heart   could   still   fall   as   hard ____ at   twen - ty - three. ____
smile's   for - ev - er   in   my   mind   and   mem - o - ry. ____

And   I'm   think - ing 'bout   how ____
And   I'm   think - ing 'bout   how ____

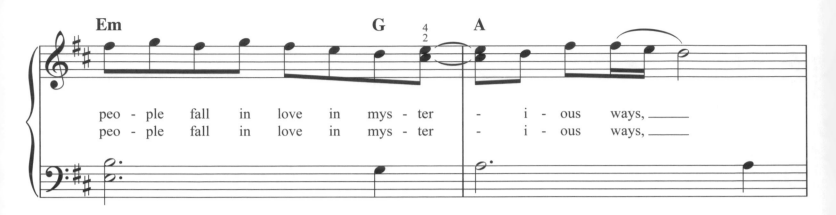

peo - ple fall in love in mys - ter - i - ous ways, _____
peo - ple fall in love in mys - ter - i - ous ways, _____

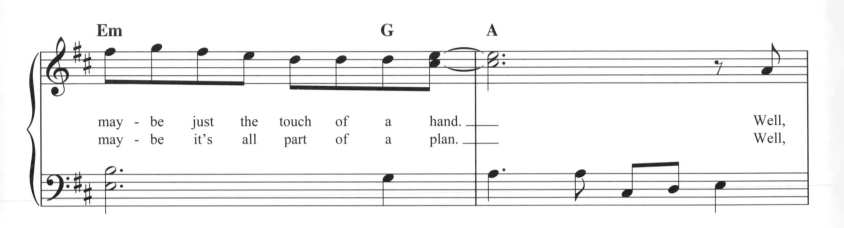

may - be just the touch of a hand. _____ Well,
may - be it's all part of a plan. _____ Well,

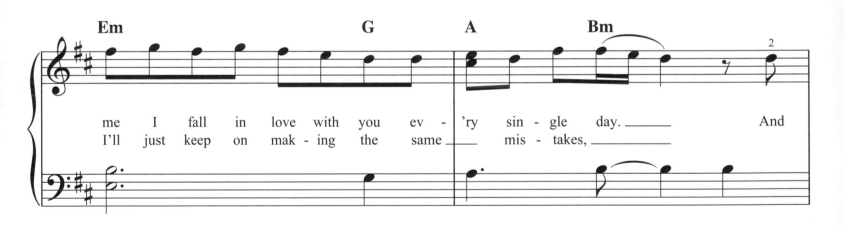

me I fall in love with you ev - 'ry sin - gle day. _____ And
I'll just keep on mak - ing the same ____ mis - takes, _____

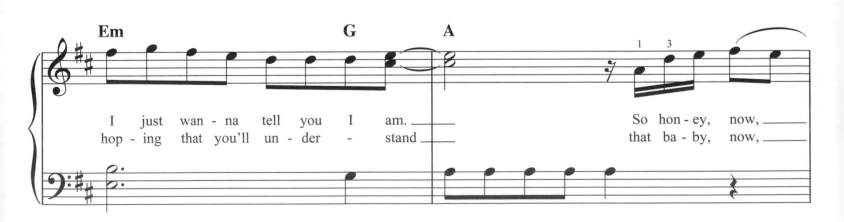

I just wan - na tell you I am. _____ So hon - ey, now, _____
hop - ing that you'll un - der - stand ____ that ba - by, now, _____

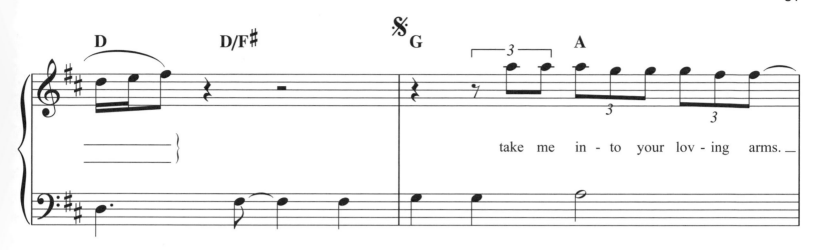

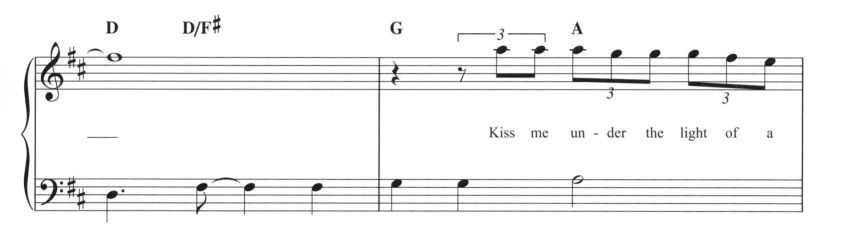

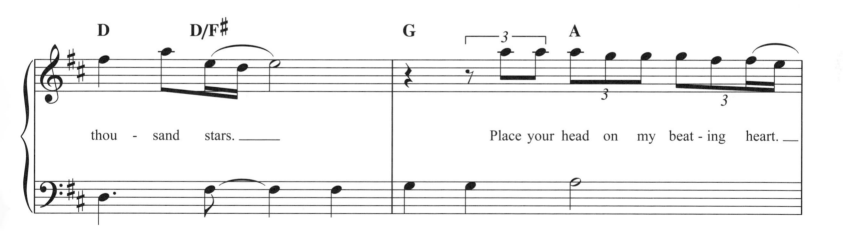

Solo ends So, ba - by, now, _____

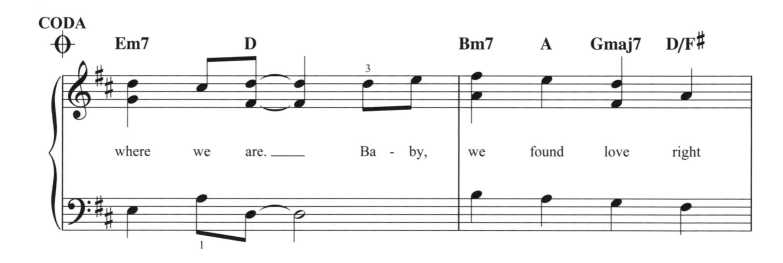

where we are. _____ Ba - by, we found love right

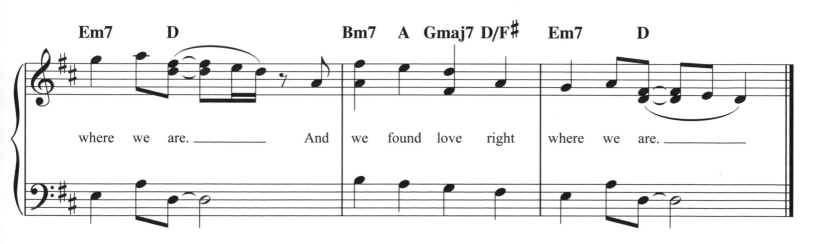

where we are. _____ And we found love right where we are. _____

RISE UP

Words and Music by CASSANDRA BATIE
and JENNIFER DECILVEO

C

you, _____ for you,

G

Am

you, _____ for

F   D.C. al Coda

you. _____

CODA   **F**

___ times a - gain ____ for

C

you, _____ for you, _____

G

Am

you, _____ for

F

you. _____

C

All   we need,   all we   need is   hope. ___ And for that we have

G

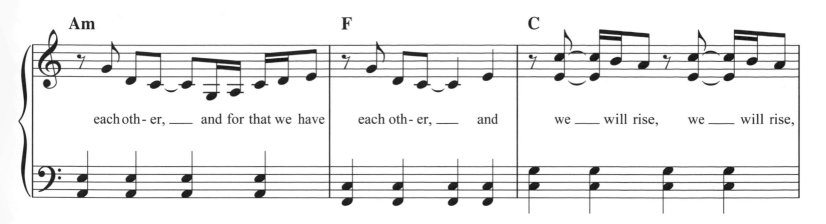

each oth- er, ___ and for that we have each oth- er, ___ and we __ will rise, we __ will rise,

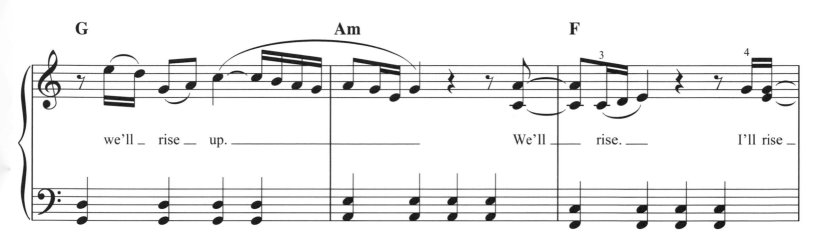

we'll _ rise _ up. _____ We'll ___ rise. __ I'll rise _

__ up, I'll rise __ like the day. _ I'll rise up in __ spite of the ache.

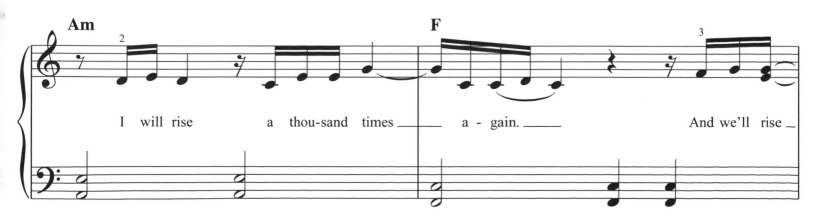

I will rise a thou-sand times ___ a - gain. __ And we'll rise _

up high like the waves. We'll rise up in spite of the ache. We'll rise

up and we'll do it a thou-sand times a-gain for

you, for you, you, for

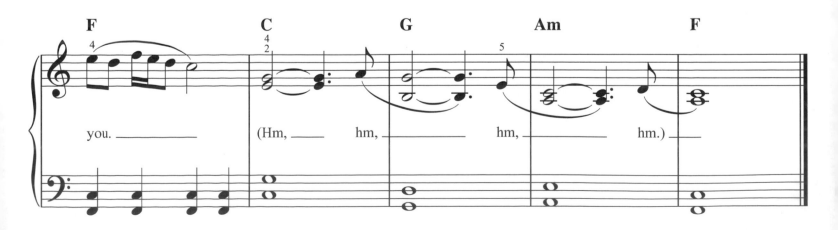

you. (Hm, hm, hm, hm.)